GAMES YOU CAN PLAY
WITH YOUR
PUSSY

Written By:
Muffy Winthrope

Illustrated By:
Martin Riskin

© 1993
by **Ivory Tower Publishing Company, Inc.**
All Rights Reserved

No portion of this book may be reproduced - mechanically, electronically, or by any other means including photocopying - without the permission of the publisher.

Manufactured in the United States of America

30 29 28 27 26 25 24 23 22 21 20 19 18 17 16 15 14 13 12 11 10 9 8 7 6 5 4 3 2 1

Ivory Tower Publishing Co., Inc.
125 Walnut St., P.O. Box 9132, Watertown, MA 02272-9132
Telephone #: (617) 923-1111   Fax #: (617) 923-8839

WHY EVERYONE SHOULD HAVE A PUSSY

Pussies make great pets. They make better pets than gorillas, anyway. Can you imagine a pussy eating a banana and swinging from the shower curtain and beating its little chest and making faces at strangers? And pussies certainly are better pets than hippopotamuses. Pussies don't spend all day in the bathtub with just their noses above water. And they don't have great, ugly mouths with only two great ugly teeth in them. They have cut little mouths, with sharp little teeth in them which they use only when provoked or when they just feel like biting you.

Who can argue that pussies are not better pets than turkeys? Pussies do not strut and look goofy and gobble. Pussies peep and they meow and they sing like old ladies, but they never gobble. Pussies are better pets than porcupines, for example, and skunks and moles and raccoons and beavers and woodchucks and squirrels and chipmunks, all for reasons too obvious to mention.

WHY EVERYONE SHOULD HAVE A PUSSY

Ditto for lions and tigers and elephants and three-toed sloths and polar bears and anteaters and snakes (especially snakes) and big things that go crunch in the night.

And don't forget coyotes and wolves and antelopes and buffalo and brown bears and pumas and zebras (only because what goes with stripes?) and donkeys and most horses and certain rabbits named Gus. I think that only leaves scorpions and all bugs and birds and everything else we have not named. And dogs.

About dogs. I wouldn't give you an old box of Milkbones and six pieces of panda poop for the finest dog that ever lived. But I would kill for a little pussy.

NAMING YOUR PUSSY

It is important for you to realize just how crucial choosing a name for your pussy can be. It sets the whole tone for the animal's existence. Picking the incorrect name can be a devastating and permanently traumatic experience for pussy. Imagine a 29-pound tom with the name "Llewelyn" or a fluffy, white angora called "Scarface."

Don't rush into a name choice. Study your pussy's personality; watch it at play; judge its habits. Then select something that really fits.

To help with this sometimes difficult task, we have compiled a list of names for cute, cuddly pussies, and a list of names for aggressive, independent pussies.

NAMING YOUR PUSSY

Cute, Cuddly Pussy Names

Muffy
Boots
Mr. Whiskers
Sunshine
Freckles
Snowball
Molly
Pumpkin
Chester
Silly
Heather

Aggressive, Independent Pussy Names

Hairball
Edward Wellington Mouseripper
Ghengis Cat
Alexander the Hairy
Fatty Mousebuckle
Katmandu
Slink
Black Jack
Miss Kitty
Nervous Norman
Lightnin'

NAMING YOUR PUSSY

If none of these names seems to fit try selecting any name from Column A and combining it with any name from Column B.

Column A

    Willy
    Daisy
    Mirabel
    Fluffy
    Peanut
    Bibs
    Taffy
    Clover

Column B

Hot Pants
Winston Church Cat
Nymph
Tom Cat
Delight
Galore
Ballou
Lover

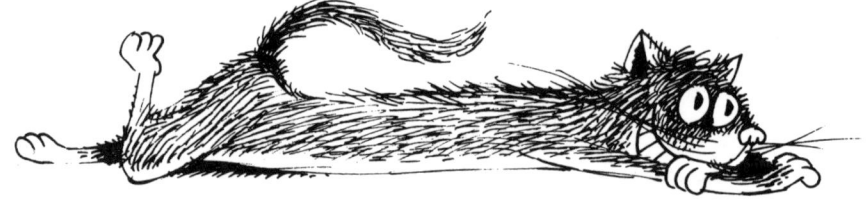

HOW TO FEED YOUR PUSSY

"How to feed your pussy" is a whole lot different than "What to feed your pussy." Because if they are in the mood, the hairy little beggars will eat until they puff up like adders and their eyes fall out. If they are not in the mood, they will not eat anything at all. For days. This section really ought to be called "Getting your pussy in the mood," but that's another story altogether.

Experts tell us there are two ways to cope with recalcitrant pussies when it comes to feeding: the Ess, Ess, Mine Pussy approach; and the Up-Your-Nose-With-A-Rubber-Hose approach.

HOW TO FEED YOUR PUSSY

The Ess, Ess Mine Pussy Approach

Pussy has not eaten in three days, and you are dreadfully worried. What if the cute little thing faints from hunger in the middle of the street and the neighbors find it and accuse you of being a bad cook. Or it starts hallucinating and runs away with a pussy from the wrong side of the tracks. What to do, what to do? Simple. Prepare every dish you can think of, no matter what the cost, and lock your pussy in a room with all the food, all the while talking to it in coaxing, motherly tones. Later, when you unlock the door, the cat will have tipped over all the bowls and everything will have run together in a big, disgusting, smelly mess. But not to worry. While pussy is polishing off a pouch of dry food, you can serve it to your husband Morris and tell him it's a new recipe for goulash.

HOW TO FEED YOUR PUSSY

The Up-Your-Nose-With-A-Rubber-Hose Approach

Pussy has not eaten in three days, and frankly you don't give a damn. You hope the little pest faints from hunger in the middle of the street and is run over by a Mack truck. Or is dragged to Tiajuana by the boxer next door and left there with child. But your kids are crying and whining and begging you to make things okay. So you put on work pants, a flannel shirt and heavy gloves and close yourself in a room with the cat, a steel funnel and three pounds of dry pet food. Holding the squirming pussy firmly between your knees, you force the funnel into its mouth and start to pour in the nourishment. Later, when the deep scratch that runs from your eyebrow to your ankle heals, you will be arrested for trying to burn down the ASPCA.

HOW TO EAT WITH YOUR PUSSY

Many people who have pussies feed them separately rather than with the rest of the family. And it's no wonder. We have been brainwashed to believe that pussies should be fed on the floor from plastic dishes—just think back to all the pictures you've ever seen of pussies eating or to television commercials for cat food—and not at the table like human beings, which pussies would be if they weren't cats.

Eating with your pussy can be a great deal of fun, if you are willing to accept the fact that in the beginning, the cat is going to walk in a few salads and bat a few spare ribs onto the floor. But honestly, it'll all be worth it, once you teach the cute little critter the rudiments of etiquette.

HOW TO EAT WITH YOUR PUSSY

The Rudiments of Etiquette:

Here are some rules you should make sure your pussy learns if it is going to have its own little chair and its own little silverware and its own little place at the table.

1. Keep your hind feet off the table.
2. It's okay to play with your food; don't play with mine.
3. Don't drag greasy food onto the floor unless you have permission; I'm never going to give you permission.
4. It's all right to wash your hands and face at the table after eating but save the more private parts until everyone else has finished eating.
5. Don't look at me like that; I'm not giving you any more prime rib.

PUSSY HAIRS

Face facts. You have a pussy. A pussy has hair. Therefore, you are going to have pussy hairs in or on everything you own.

When you get up in the morning and sit down to breakfast, you will discover pussy hairs in your coffee. When you get dressed to go to work, you will discover pussy hairs on your trousers. When you take out your hanky to blow your nose, more pussy hairs.

You will have pussy hairs on your carpet, pussy hairs on your favorite chair, pussy hairs on all your clothes and pussy hairs in everything you eat.

PUSSY HAIRS

And that's not the worst part. When you sit down to supper at the end of a long day and you can't find the pussy hair, you will get very nervous. You know it's there someplace, and you sure as hell don't want to eat it. So you spend the entire meal examining every forkful of food very carefully, holding it up to the light, studying it for the telltale wisp. Finally, your dinner ruined and your stomach sour, you go into the next room for a smoke, stick a cigarette into your mouth, and, just as you are about to light it, discover something under your tongue. A pussy hair.

PUSSY HAIRS

While you can never eliminate them completely, there are some steps you can take to keep the pussy hair situation under control.

Brushing Your Pussy: Do this at least twice a day. Buy a stiff bristled brush and stroke your pussy up and down at least 100 times. After you do this for three or four days, your pussy will have shiny, glossy coat and you will have collected enough hair to stuff a mattress the size of British Columbia.

Vacuuming Your Pussy: This is for people who don't have enough time to brush their pussies. Stand on your pussy's tail to keep it from a) running away and b) being sucked into the vacuum cleaner. Your pussy will not like this at first. Give it a little time. Later, he will learn to hate it.

PUSSY HAIRS

Shellacking Your Pussy: If you don't have the time to groom your pussy every day, this is a practical if somewhat extreme way of keeping all the pussy hairs where they belong: on the pussy. It has other advantages as well. Instead of having to let the little critter out at night, you can just lean it in a corner. Or, use it as a doorstop.

PUSSY POO-POO

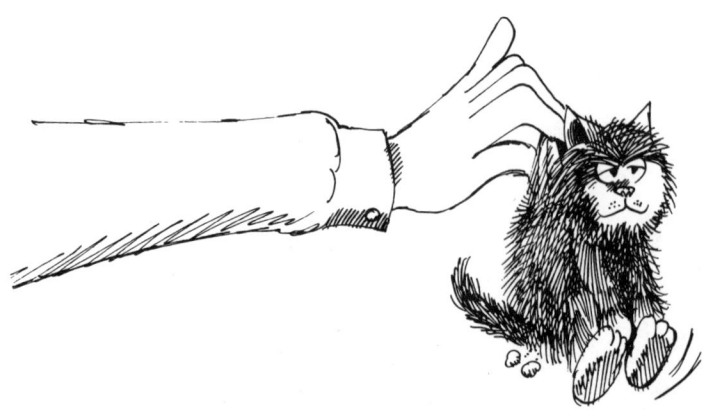

Pussy poo-poo is the most unpleasant thing about having a pussy. It goes in as tuna and cream but it comes out as something that's responsible for a lot of air fresheners being sold.

But poo-poo is one of those unpleasant facts of life, like taxes and recycling the aluminum trays from your Chinese take-out, so you're just going to have to learn to deal with it.

Dealing With It: One thing about cats. They are creatures of habit. If a cat makes a poo-poo in a corner once, it will make poo-poos there for the rest of its life. So make sure your pussy starts poo-pooing where you want it to poo-poo, and not, say, in your loafers. Otherwise, you will spend a lot of time washing your socks.

Now, once your pussy starts to poo-poo, you'll want to put something under it to poo-poo into. Which brings us to...

PUSSY POO-POO

The Litter Box: Litter boxes come in two sizes. Too small and too large. The ones that are too small force your pussy to make poo-poo and wee-wee over the sides of the box, thereby negating the box's worth. The ones that are too large look empty unless they have 25 pounds of litter in them, thereby making your litter bill equivalent to your weekly food bill. Litter boxes are made from three materials: plastic, which costs a whole lot more than you can imagine; cardboard, which sags when it gets wet; and foil, which pussies like to rip up so any excess fluids can escape. None solve the worst problem of the smell.

PUSSY POO-POO

The Smell: There is nothing you can do about the smell. You can put baking soda in with the litter if you want to find little white pussy tracks all over the house later. You can try building an enclosure over the top of the litter box and thereby release all the smell at once every time you change the litter. You can even try putting perfume into your pussy's food. It won't work either. Just resign yourself to the fact that you can never have guests in your home again.

PUSSY POO-POO

When To Change The Litter: Since you yourself will have long lost your own sense of smell, you should look for indications for when it's time to change the litter. Are insects dropping from the air? Is your pussy spending a lot of time with its legs crossed because it's too disgusted to go in there again? Have they tacked a "quarantined" sign to the side of your house?

Alternatives: Teach your pussy to use the toilet. You use the toilet at the corner gas station. Have your pussy surgically altered so it never makes poo-poo, then watch it blow up like a balloon.

SLEEPING WITH YOUR PUSSY

Pussies are warm and cuddly and generally fun to snuggle with. You probably know that already.

You probably also know that even though they are warm and cuddly, sometimes they are not fun to sleep with. That is because they are nocturnal animals and like to wait until you are on the verge of sleep before starting to clean themselves and race around trying to catch their tails and dragging dead cigarette butts and other little surprises into bed to bury under the sheets.

SLEEPING WITH YOUR PUSSY

And every time you wake up and try to catch them so you can throw them through the window, they race under the bed and hide there until you give up and are on the verge of sleep again, then race out and begin all over.

When the hairy little beggar finally does settle down (usually about the first light), it decides to do it in the exact middle of the bed so you cannot stretch your legs, or on your pillow so every time you roll over, you get a mouth full of hairs.

SLEEPING WITH YOUR PUSSY

But let's take it one problem at a time. Your first is getting your pussy to settle down.

Getting Your Pussy To Settle Down: Of course, the easy way out is to put sleeping pills into your pussy's midnight snack. In fact, short of wrapping your pussy in a size 11 black sock, this is the only way out. Do it. But don't let your pussy have a nightcap. It could be dangerous.

SLEEPING WITH YOUR PUSSY

Positioning Your Pussy: Once your pussy has settled down, you have to decide where to put it in bed. In the middle is no good and on the pillow is no good, both for reasons already mentioned. Under the pillow might be okay, except if the sleeping pill wears off before you wake up, pussy will think it is in an Edgar Allan Poe story and go bananas, probably clawing your face down to your brains trying to escape. You do not want this to happen. Under the covers is no good for the same reason.

The only solution, really, is to buy a big basket and put a soft pad in it and sleep in there and let pussy sleep wherever it wants.

YOUR PUSSY AND YOUR FURNITURE

One of the biggest problems pussy owners have is what pussies do to furniture. They scratch it and tear it and rip the stuffing out of it. They lie on it and roll around on it and leave hairs all over it. They walk on it instead of walking on the floor and they bury little surprises behind the cushions and they think it is a swell place to leave hairballs.

No one has yet come up with a fool-proof solution to the problem, but there are some tried and true alternatives that do work. Sometimes.

YOUR PUSSY AND YOUR FURNITURE

Teaching Your Pussy To Respect Your Furniture: If you have an intelligent pussy, this is an approach that has a lot of merit. Bring home furniture catalogs and show your pussy that the couch it is currently tearing the stuffing out of is now selling for $1495 plus tax. Repeat the lesson for the end table with the gouges and the love seat with the vomit stain. If you do not seem to be getting through, bring out a catalog of pussy coffins and point out how much more inexpensive they are than your furniture. This has been know to kindle the light of understanding in more than one pussy.

YOUR PUSSY AND YOUR FURNITURE

Reasoning With Your Pussy: Sometime after dinner during the mellow part of the evening, invite your pussy into the library for some brandy and cigars. While you are both sitting and reflecting quietly about life, puffing on your Havanas and sipping your Hennesssey Four-Star, trying not to look at the rip in your new $9000 leather arm chair, ask your pussy if it thinks it is fair for one of you to work and slave so that the other can spend its time destroying everything in the house. Talk rationally about the need for civility and respect for property. Say that you know things can be worked out if only certain pussies would try. Be sober and straightforward and sincere. If that doesn't work, trick your pussy into tearing the "Do Not Remove This Tag Under Penalty of Law" tag off of the sofa, then turn him in.

YOUR PUSSY AND YOUR FURNITURE

Stuffing Your Furniture Into The Closet: Every time you go out of the house or leave the room, stuff your furniture into the closet.

Stuffing Your Pussy Into The Closet: Every time you go out of the house or leave the room, stuff your pussy into the closet.

Buying Cement Furniture: Buy cement furniture. It does not collect hair and cannot have the stuffing torn out of it, since it is the stuffing. This is only good if you live on the ground floor.

Putting Your Pussy In A Plastic Bag: This approach has its drawbacks. It's no fun having a pussy if you can't take it out and play with it. However, this approach also has its advantages. It tends to keep all the loose hair in one place. But you decide what's more important to you. A neat pussy, or a breathing pussy.

YOUR PUSSY AND YOUR FERN

Many people who have a pussy also have a fern. It is not as unusual as you might think. What is unusual, though, is finding a way to get your pussy to leave your fern alone.

Pussies like to play with ferns, and they like to eat them, too. They shred the poor fern's leaves and bite off the poor fern's stems, and pretty soon the fern is all brown and shriveled and not much good to anyone anymore.

How to keep your pussy away from your fern? Good question. Here are 5 possible answers.

YOUR PUSSY AND YOUR FERN

Change Your Pussy's Diet: What your pussy is trying to tell you is that it wants more greens in its diet. This is mainly a problem with indoor rather than outdoor pussies, who can molest ferns at will. Try giving it some chopped lettuce with its dinner. Better still, plant some grass in an indoor planter. That way, pussy can have an appetizer before it gets down to the serious business of eating your fern.

Make Your Fern Seem Less Appealing: One way to keep pussy at bay is to doctor your fern to make it seem less desirable. Try painting it orange. Or smearing it with succotash. Pussies hate succotash. Use your imagination. If you were a pussy, what would make you lose interest in a fern?

YOUR PUSSY AND YOUR FERN

Make Your Fern Less Accessible: If your pussy can't get at it, your fern will be safe from damage. So try suspending it from the ceiling, too high for your pussy to jump up to. Or lock it in the wine cabinet. Or take a picture of it and send the fern to your mother's, then put the picture where the fern used to be. Your pussy will eat the picture by mistake and get a tummy ache and learn a valuable lesson.

Buy Your Fern Some Protection: Go to a place that sells exotic plants and buy a Venus Pussy Eater. Put it next to your fern. This is cruel but can be effective.

Alternatively, stick your pussy's tail into an electrical socket.

YOUR PUSSY AND YOUR FERN

Alter Your Pussy's Behavior Patterns: Teach your pussy that eating your fern is not a good thing. Teach it this by saying a loud word every time you see your pussy eating your fern. If this does not work and you start getting hoarse, try switching to a loud sound to scare your pussy away. If this does not work, cover your pussy with mayonnaise and put it between two slices of bread. Say you want to show it what it feels like to be eaten. Depending on how far you wish to carry the charade, this could end the problem once and for all.

DISCIPLINING YOUR PUSSY

Sometimes pussy gets a little too rambunctious and needs to be taught a lesson. There are two extremes in disciplining your pussy.

At one end of the scale is saying "Tsk, tsk" and sighing heavily. At the other end is tying your pussy into a canvas sack with the first nine volumes of the encyclopedia and dropping it into 11 feet of cold water.

But there is no reason to lay a major hurt on your pussy—until you have exhausted all other avenues.

DISCIPLINING YOUR PUSSY

All Other Avenues: One way to discipline your pussy is to use the Pavlovian or classical method. You'll remember that Pavlov trained his dog to salivate every time the dog heard a bell ring. So every time your pussy does something wrong, ring a bell, and Pavlov's dog will come over and salivate on it.

Another popular method is to alter your pussy's patterns if it falls into bad habits. By altering behavior patterns, you are really altering the way your pussy thinks. Some people say the best way to do this is to correct pussy every time it does something you do not want it to do by showing it the right thing to do. Repetition will eventually produce a pussy who says "Duh," and shadow boxes a lot.

NURSING A SICK PUSSY

Nothing looks quite so sad as a sick pussy. The spunk, the vitality, the old get up and go have all got up and gone. Now pussy is a sorry looking creature indeed.

You ask yourself, "How can I tell if my pussy is really sick?"

There are many ways. Give $42 to a veterinarian to do it for you. Throw a live tuna fish on the floor and study pussy's reaction. If there isn't any, chances are something's wrong.

Ask your pussy, "Are you sick?"

Once you have got your answer, take some action.

NURSING A SICK PUSSY

Some Action: Make sure pussy is as comfy-cozy as possible. Put it on a fluffy bed of pillows in a room with lots of lace curtains and calico. Give it sweet cream and talk to it in baby talk and make it a cute little pair of pajamas. This should make your pussy throw up and feel better.

Some More Action: Leave pussy alone. Nature has provided its own devices for taking care of sick animals. So just let nature take its course. Unless pussy comes to you and asks for some penicillin.

Watching Pussy's Diet: When it is under the weather, pussy will not eat what it usually eats. It will want a more bland diet. So cut out the chili peppers and 10-year-old Scotch. Not to mention the rich sauces and heavy desserts.

Your Bedside Manner: Your bedside manner is very important. Try not to be boisterous or too cheerful. Don't blow cigar smoke in pussy's face or stay too long and make yourself unwelcome. Be somber but solicitous. Quiet decorum is in order. Remember, in their hearts, most pussies are Presbyterians.

HOW TO HANDLE A HOT PUSSY

Okay. It's time to get frank. Every once in a while, if you have not had it "fixed," your pussy is going to get "urges."

You may notice these "urges," because pussy will be bouncing off the walls and howling and sliding up and down the bannisters. If you do not have bannisters, pussy will be sliding up and down your leg. These "urges" are only nature's way of telling pussy it is time to get some. If pussy cannot get some, that is bad news. It will get cross and erratic and pass remarks about your relationship with your mother.

For reasons of your own, though, you might not want pussy to have some. Perhaps you do not want your house littered with kittens. Perhaps you are not getting any yourself and don't see any reason why your pussy should. Whatever, you should be prepared for dealing with the hots.

HOW TO HANDLE A HOT PUSSY

Dealing With The Hots: Recognize that pussy is suffering extreme physical and mental anguish. Try coping with these problems separately. To deal with the physical, keep your pussy in a dark closet until the urges seem to pass. To deal with the mental, keep shouting into the dark closet that if the cat doesn't stop whining, you are never going to let it out.

Being Reasonable: This approach may seem harsh to you. If so, try being reasonable. Try telling your pussy that it is not in its best interests to have its normal, biological needs satisfied. When you both stop laughing, stun it with a two-pound tube of K-Y lubricant, then lock it in a dark closet.

Preventive Action: Here, you have decided to accept the inevitable. The call of nature is too strong, and pussy is going to find a way to have it satisfied. So sit down and have a person-to-pussy talk about contraceptive devices. Maybe you can learn something.

PUSSY HYGIENE—HOW TO GIVE YOUR PUSSY A BATH

Many people think pussies are clean animals, equating the feline oral fixation with sanitation. We do not know what you call an animal that spends its time having its body tongued, but where we come from, we do not call it sanitary. Dirty and perverse, perhaps, but not sanitary.

Pussies, like dust mops, are fuzzy and collect loose dirt. Licking at the filth only gives them unbearable breath and coats the color of mud, which means bathing at least once a week.

PUSSY HYGIENE—HOW TO GIVE YOUR PUSSY A BATH

Now, it is well known how pussies feel about water. They don't mind looking, but they hate to touch. There are many documented cases of pussies falling into water-filled bathtubs and escaping without getting wet.

Herewith, then, is a simple guide to giving your pussy a bath, which, if followed to the letter, will result in a great deal of pain and disappointment for everyone.

STEP ONE: Fill the bathtub with scalding water. By the time you get your pussy into the tub, the water temperature will be comfortable. If not, having your pussy neutered will no longer be a problem.

PUSSY HYGIENE—HOW TO GIVE YOUR PUSSY A BATH

STEP TWO: Lay out all the supplies you are going to need: soap, sponge, washcloth, scrub-brush, iodine, gauze, band-aids, vaseline, rubber gloves, plunger, whip, chair, pistol, mace and pussy dictionary turned to the phrase "Mommy, mommy, mommy." Pray.

PUSSY HYGIENE—HOW TO GIVE YOUR PUSSY A BATH

STEP THREE: Now it's time to get your pussy's confidence. Take it to a movie; buy it a malted; treat it to an all-night session at a people house. Talk to it quietly; pet it on the neck and show it pictures of chickens. Then, when your pussy is good and relaxed, when its mind is at ease, and it's purring and drowsy and content, strike it in the forehead with a monkey wrench.

STEP FOUR: Carry the limp pussy to the tub and place it gently on a bath mat. Working quickly, smear the sides of the tub with vaseline so the pussy will not be able to claw its way out once immersed. Test the temperature of the water by holding the pussy's head in the shallow end. This will do two things. It will revive your pussy. It will invest it with the fear of God.

PUSSY HYGIENE—HOW TO GIVE YOUR PUSSY A BATH

STEP FIVE: Put your pussy completely in the water. This is sometimes done more easily by placing a jukebox on the bridge of its nose. Stroke your pussy gently during what will be a first few seconds of berserk insanity. If it does not calm down after a few moments, smack it sharply in the groin.

STEP SIX: Try stroking your pussy with a soapy sponge. If your pussy is still a bit tense and indicates its discomfort by, say, opening a running wound from your eyebrow to your elbow, dump a cup of laundry detergent into the water. Then, using an electric mixer, beat the water at medium speed, scraping the sides of the tub occasionally to make sure the pussy is evenly mixed. When you finish, you will have a hairball the size of Cleveland.

PUSSY HYGIENE—HOW TO GIVE YOUR PUSSY A BATH

STEP SEVEN: Using the same wrist action you would employ to throw a hard slider, snatch your soaked pussy from the water by taking its tail and whipping it smartly about your head until it is barely damp. Then throw it into a dryer with the controls set for "wool." While your pussy is being fluff-dried, take two aspirin and have someone you love give you a back rub.

STEP EIGHT: Buy yourself a dog.

PUTTING YOUR PUSSY IN THE KENNEL

We all know that pussies hate being confined in small places. They love to be able to curl up in a tight ball in the middle of a large bed.

In kennels, all they have are small places. There is no room to curl up in a tight ball in the middle of a large bed. There is only room to curl up in a tight ball in the middle of a small cage. There is not a pussy alive who doesn't know this. There is not a pussy alive who will go to a kennel without a fight—unless you know how to trick it.

PUTTING YOUR PUSSY IN THE KENNEL
How To Trick It

Be nonchalant— Be nonchalant. Whistle a carefree tune, walk casually past your pussy and bend down to scratch it behind the ear. When your pussy is relaxed, ram it into a shoe box, wrap the box with heavy twine and speed off to the kennel. Don't worry about putting air holes in the box. Pussy will make its own.

Be honest—Sit down for a person-to-pussy talk. Make the assumption that your pussy can be reasonable if you are reasonable. Tell pussy where you are going to take it. By the time you get your pussy out from inside the sofa, you will realize that honesty never solved anything.

PUTTING YOUR PUSSY IN THE KENNEL
How To Trick It

Be underhanded—Tell your pussy you are going to make it feel good. Tell it you are going to take it to a place where they specialize in making pussies feel good. Tell it you think it should loosen up before it goes to this place, and give it a glass of straight Scotch laced with Pussy-Go-Nap. When your pussy wakes up, you will be in Barbados.

Be mean—Hire two men to get your pussy to the kennel, no matter what. No questions asked. Tell your pussy you have hired two men to take it to the kennel, no matter what. No questions asked. It will help if these men have colorful names, like Muscular Vito and Not-Known-For-His-Compassion Nick. Your pussy will run for its life, followed by these two men. Who knows. There may be a television series here.

PUSSY GIVES YOU A GIFT

What pussy owner has never received a gift from his or her pussy? Like a dead moth or a gnarled flower. Or a half-eaten mouse. Or the stuffing from your favorite chair.

Perhaps you never considered these things to be gifts, just pussy yucch. But think about this for a moment. When a pussy wants to express feelings of affection for its owner, it can't whip out a Mastercharge and run down to Saks. It must rely on the resources of its own cunning. So a dead mouse on your doorstep says, "I love you." Unless you have a Sicilian pussy. Then it means, "Say your prayers, fettucini face."

In truth, most people are puzzled by gifts. They don't know what to make of them.

PUSSY GIVES YOU A GIFT

What to make of them

Here is a list of things your pussy is likely to bring you and what they mean.

A Dead Mouse
1. I love you.
2. I hope you find this in the morning after a greasy breakfast 'cause I love to watch you throw up.

A Dead Bird
1. Catching a bird is a feat of great prowess. I did it for you because I love you.
2. I found this in the street. Throw it away, will you, old man? The smell is making me nauseous.

PUSSY GIVES YOU A GIFT

What to make of them

Stuffing From Your Favorite Chair
1. I opened a new present for you. And there's more where that came from. I love you.
2. Look what I found. I tried to put it back, but I couldn't. Why don't you stuff it?

A Dead Dog
1. I am mighty and will protect you against all intruders. I love you.
2. I fixed old Bowser's ass. And I can fix yours, too. Remember that the next time you're too tired to get up and let me out in the middle of the night.

A Dead Mailman
1. Whoops.
2. Whoops.

HOW TO GET YOUR PUSSY OUT OF A TREE

Cats like to climb. It is God's way. But while God made cats very fond of going up, he did not make them all that crazy about coming down. Let's face it. Your basic pussy is no dope. It is cruising down the street about 90 miles-per-hour in front of some big Irish Setter and sees an old oak, and before you can say "Holy Mother......ape.......," it is clinging to the very end branch of the very top limb of the tree. Breathing real hard. And happy to be safe. Then comes a big mistake. Your pussy looks down. How can I describe fear? Picture if you will your own wedding night.

If you were watching all of this, you'd say, "The cat has a problem." But you'd be wrong, litter breath. You have a problem. Your kids will begin to cry and the neighbors will gather around and look concerned and people will begin to murmur things like "...sissy," and "...ought to be ashamed," and "...maybe we ought to string him up." You know what your problem is? How to get your pussy out of a tree.

HOW TO GET YOUR PUSSY OUT OF A TREE

People who know about these things—all of them are deceased—say there are three ways to get your pussy out of a tree. First, you can try to...

Coax It Down: Tell the pussy you are an Irish priest named Father Murphy. Speaking in a soft brogue, you tell the quivering critter that, sure, he's going to get sent to the Big House, but the warden's a friend of yours, and that with a good word from the governor and with time off for good behavior, he ought to be out in twenty or thirty years. Then sing a chorus of "Danny Boy."

While you are drying off the top of your head, think about resorting to more direct means like...

HOW TO GET YOUR PUSSY OUT OF A TREE

Throwing Things At Your Pussy: Don't throw anything that will do real damage. The cat will probably march down and give you five across your lips, then lay you open like a big wheel of cheese. No, no. Loft soft things into the tree, like marshmallows and veiled threats and pictures of the veterinarian's office where you will surely take pussy if it doesn't stop making you look like a jerk.

HOW TO GET YOUR PUSSY OUT OF A TREE

Go Up The Tree Yourself: If you do this thing, you will die. So don't do this thing. Unless the picture of a helpless, frightened, crying little kitty cat upsets you, forget all about this.

The first thing you will need will be a ladder. Then a heavy shirt and heavy pants and heavy shoes and heavy socks and heavy gloves and a heavy hat and a heavy friend to hold the ladder. Then you will need rope and a net and iodine and band-aids and some lunch for you and some lunch for your pussy and a ball point pen and a piece of paper which says "I will never do this again" and which you will make your pussy sign before you help it out of the tree. Then you will need someone there who can call the fire department to come and get you both out of the tree.

EXERCISING YOUR PUSSY

They took a poll once to find out what people hate the most. And do you know what finished right behind taxes and the metric system? Flabby pussies. Yes, all of us agree there is nothing much more useless than a flabby pussy. Pussies ought to be sleek and firm and taut and sinuous. They ought to be. Sometimes they are not. You can fix that, though, by exercising your pussy. Here are a few regimens.

EXERCISING YOUR PUSSY

A Few Regimens

Running Your Pussy Ragged: You may not want to run yourself ragged while you are running your pussy ragged. Running may disagree with you. Tie your pussy to the crosstown bus. That ought to get the job done.

Limbering Up Your Pussy: Before you exercise your pussy, you will probably want to limber it up. Don't. There is nothing more difficult to catch than a limber pussy.

EXERCISING YOUR PUSSY

A Few Regimens

Stretching Your Pussy: Stretch your pussy instead of limbering it up. You can do it by hand or by utilizing a mechanical device. Whatever seems to work best. A stretched pussy is a loose pussy. A loose pussy is a relaxed pussy. A relaxed pussy is a healthy pussy. Except when it is flabby.

EXERCISING YOUR PUSSY

A Few Regimens

Making Your Pussy Muscular: You can make your pussy muscular if you want by making it do sit-ups, push-ups, jumping jacks, deep knee bends, toe raises and running in place, to say nothing of pumping Friskies. But you might be interested to know that they took a poll once to find out what people hate the most. And do you know what finished right behind getting old and chewing aluminum? Muscular pussies.

TALKING WITH YOUR PUSSY

Actually, this section ought to be called, "Trying To Get Your Pussy To Talk Back." For there is nothing unusual about people talking to their pussies. It is done all the time. People do it because they are lonely ("What did you do Saturday night?" "Oh, nothing. I just sat in the corner and talked to my pussy.") or because they have no one better to talk to ("Hello, pretty baby. Don't you look beautiful tonight." "Thanks, George." "Back off, Selma, I was talking to the cat.") or because they love their pussy ("Oh, God, I love my pussy.")

The secret is in trying to get your pussy to talk back. Now, before you are consumed by waves of doubt, let me be quick to point out that the occurrence is not unprecedented. Many pussy owners have succeeded in establishing a meaningful dialogue with their little hairy friends. It's just a question of knowing how to go about it.

TALKING WITH YOUR PUSSY

How To Go About It

You may not think this is going to work, but all I can say is try it.

Roll a cucumber in yeast, then stroke it gently but firmly until it gets warm and moist and begins to rise. Rub the turgid tuber with cat nip, then smear on a greasy unguent and pack the practically pulsating pickle in a pint of peach preserves. Wave the warm concoction under your pussy's nose so that it understands what's at stake here, then gently suggest to the quivering creature that unless it makes with a few choice sentences, you're going to stick it in her ear. All I can say is, you'll be surprised at what happens.

GAMES YOU CAN PLAY WITH YOUR PUSSY

Pussy Pong

A favorite pussy trick is to creep up on the table and hide behind the net and make funny faces at you while you serve.

Another is to run off with the ball whenever they get a one-point lead.

GAMES YOU CAN PLAY WITH YOUR PUSSY

Five Card Pussy

In this test of skill and nerve, it is likely your pussy will humiliate you. They love to say, "Look at the mouse," and when your back is turned, peek at your cards.

GAMES YOU CAN PLAY WITH YOUR PUSSY

Pussy Of The Mountain

Your pussy is on top of the hill and you have to throw your pussy off. Bring band-aids.

GAMES YOU CAN PLAY WITH YOUR PUSSY

Kick The Pussy

Street sneakers are okay, but many prefer to play wearing sneakers. Of course, considering the object of the game, your pussy may not prefer to play at all.

Pussy Go Seek

While your pussy is counting to 100, drive to Vermont and put up with some friends.

GAMES YOU CAN PLAY WITH YOUR PUSSY

Putting With Your Pussy

This will be a snap. You think the object of the game is to put the ball into the hole. Your pussy thinks the object is to keep it out of the hole and play with it. What with bunting it with its nose and whacking it back and forth between its front paws, the score after the first hole ought to be:

You—3   Pussy—500.

GAMES YOU CAN PLAY WITH YOUR PUSSY

Pin The Tail On The Pussy

This is an old children's favorite that is starting to catch on with grown-ups. A word of caution. This game will be a lot less painful if you use scotch tape instead of thumb tacks.

GAMES YOU CAN PLAY WITH YOUR PUSSY

Spin The Pussy

A variation of the old party game. Only use your pussy instead of a bottle. And when it comes to a stop, kiss it.

GAMES YOU CAN PLAY WITH YOUR PUSSY

Musical Pussy

You have to be quick to play this game. If you sit on your pussy when the music stops, you're out.

PUSSY ZODIAC

Aries　March 21-April 19—This is a sign which bestows great strength and vitality and a love of action. Your scratch marks are deeper than anyone else's and you love to torment neighborhood dogs. Someday, they will put a price on your head.

Taurus　April 20-May 20—The emblem of earthiness rests on your proud chest, yet your actions manifest themselves in a great love of physical and material comforts. You eat like a pig and are the only cat on the block to have a charge account at Saks. You are lucky to have lived this long.

Gemini　May 21-June 21—Bright, clever and quick witted, you are nonetheless a dilettante and pip-squeak. Remember, nobody loves a wiseguy. If only you weren't so cute...

PUSSY ZODIAC

Cancer June 22-July 22—You are sociable and fond of amusement but too easily affected by the world about you. You make small children giggle and other cats purr. So why does it smell so bad after you've been in the litter box?

Leo July 23-August 22—Like your cousin the lion, you are noble, dignified and capable of rising to positions of wealth and power. You also pack a terrific right paw and have a fetish for tulips. Later, they will make a movie about your life.

Virgo August 23-September 22—You are finicky, overly fond of detail and overly critical. You will only eat certain foods, and then only when the mood strikes you. You prefer using the litter exactly 29 seconds after it's been changed and spend half your waking hours preening yourself. But you've got to stop playing with bugs.

PUSSY ZODIAC

Libra September 23-October 23—You have a deep love of order, ease and peace. Except in the middle of the night when you howl and break expensive things. You will probably wind up as a change purse.

Scorpio October 24-November 21—An extremist who is firm and obstinate, energetic and self confident. Life is a tree and you cling firmly to the top limb. What you don't know is, they've already sent for the fire department.

Sagittarius November 22-December 21—Characterized by sincerity, candor and generosity. You fall asleep a lot in the middle of dinner and like to talk to fairies. You really wish you were a bird.

PUSSY ZODIAC

Capricorn December 22-January 19—Serious, thoughtful, subtle and reserved, you will never get over the time you almost fell into the toilet. Whenever they want to know who's been tearing open the sofa, you are always asleep.

Aquarius January 20-February 18—Frequently unusual and different in either appearance, ideas or attitudes about life. The first word you ever said was, "Moo." You like having your fur stroked in the opposite direction.

Pisces February 19-March 20—The sign of the dreamer and the poet; an impractical spirit in a practical world. Everyone else looks in the mirror and sees a cat. You look into the mirror and see Muhammad Ali.

NOBODY WANTS A FAT PUSSY

Oh, they try to be brave and pretend they don't care, these owners of fat pussies. But beneath the strut and swagger, behind the brave talk and devil-may-care attitude, there is a profound yearning.

A yearning for their pussies to be slender.
To be lithe.
To be lean.

To never again have to sit on the sidelines while everyone else is playing touch football, or slow dancing, or fighting for petite sizes at bargain basement sales.

NOBODY WANTS A FAT PUSSY

Believe me. Having a fat pussy can break your heart. Hey, it's no fun walking down the street with a pussy as big as an elephant's patoot. Do people point to your pussy and guffaw?

Well, turn those guffaws into applause. Follow the advice you will find in this book and look forward to the day when you can point proudly and say, "This is *my* pussy."

HOW TO TELL IF YOUR PUSSY'S TOO FAT
10 Telltale Signs

1. Watching it breathe reminds you of a blimp rising and falling.
2. The EPA (Environmental Pussy Agency) asks you to move your pussy six inches to the right because it is making the earth tilt on its axis.
3. You press on the side of your pussy and your forefinger disappears down to the third knuckle.
4. Your pussy has a field of gravity so dense that no light escapes from it.
5. Your pussy's nickname is "Blackhole" because it sucks up any food that strays too close.

HOW TO TELL IF YOUR PUSSY'S TOO FAT

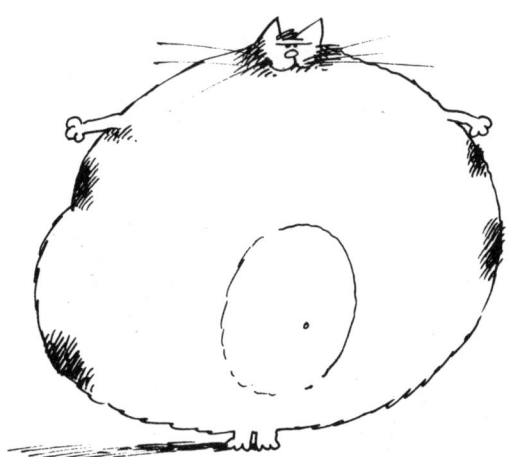

6. A Spaniard plants a flag in your pussy and claims "this new world in the name of her majesty the queen."

7. The movers say they will load your grand piano and granite block collection for free, but, want to charge triple time for handling your pussy.

8. They want you to star in a new movie called "Around My Pussy in 80 Days."

9. Arabs want to buy the mineral rights to your pussy because they figure something that big has to have oil in it somewhere.

10. They want to borrow your pussy to put on the Empire State Building so it won't blow away.

GETTING PUSSY TO FACE THE FACTS

Nobody wants to say, "Hey, look at me, I'm fat," and your pussy is no exception. "Fat" is an ugly little word, and pussies prefer not to use it.

No, pussies instead use words like "full-figured," or "mature," or "zoftig," or "short for my weight." At worst, they will admit to being "a little plump," or, occasionally, "husky." But pussies will never say they are fat. And this is the heart of the problem.

It is important to get your pussy to recognize that avoiding the truth, that trying to hide from its obesity behind a flimsy veil of semantic pretense is not going to work. You must sit down and have serious person-to-pussy talk, stressing the need for interpersonal honesty and explaining the options your portly pussy faces: diet or dismemberment.

BEGINNING THE DIET

Many pussies choose diet over dismemberment as a weight loss technique, figuring it won't hurt as much. They are wrong.

What does it mean to diet? It means giving up chocolate covered Friskies and tuna a la mode and chicken fat cocktails. It mean no more "watch me hold a turkey in my mouth" contests, speed eating beef, or taking legs of lamb to bed "to keep me company until morning." It means an end to malted milk baths, chocolate suppositories, gargling with icing, skinny-dipping in sherbet, pork chop lollypops, fudge make-up, getting naked in cream cheese, sucking on taco stands and chugging chickens. It means showing great willpower and following a strict and well monitored daily caloric intake (or giving up beverages altogether.)

PUSSY DIETS THAT REALLY WORK

There are, of course, many diets to choose from. You've got your famous Scarspussy diet, your famous Tuna Lips and water diet, your famous No-Cal Air diet, and your famous lock-up-the-refrigerator-and-send-the-key-to-a-killer-Doberman diet.

All of these are fine—if you've got the time to commit them to memory. I don't know about your pussy, but mine gets tired when it reads.

So here is a simple diet your pussy won't have any trouble following. Have your pussy's mouth wired closed and its lips sewn together. Listen we're talking serious weight loss here.

HOW TO LIVE WITH AN IRRITABLE PUSSY

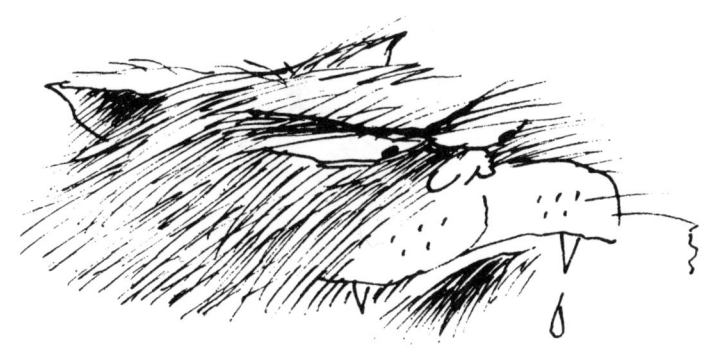

Of course, after about 10 minutes of a rigorous diet and exercise program, your pussy is going to get a little testy. It will snap at you and be most unpleasant and will gladly tear your spleen out and stuff it up your nose for a nickel.

So you must learn to live with this. You must try to humor your pussy and make nice-nice. You must live with the lights dimmed, and soft music playing, and thick carpets on the floor to deaden any unnecessary noise. You must learn to live with doors slamming, and furniture being kicked, and pussy-cursing in the middle of the night.

Take all this for about a week. Then cold-cock your pussy with the vacuum cleaner.

WHAT TO DO WITH A PUSSY WHO CHEATS

Suppose you have a pussy who is on a diet. And suppose you only feed your pussy once a day. And suppose when you feed your pussy, you only feed it tuna fish fins and cottage cheese, in other words, not very much at all. And suppose that instead of losing weight, your pussy just keeps getting heavier and heavier and heavier.

Then, my friend, it's pretty obvious. You've got a pussy who cheats. Now, a cheating pussy is no laughing matter. As country singer Hank Slim said, "A cheating pussy/will get you down/and eat your shirt/and make you frown."

If you want to stop your pussy from cheating, you've got to answer two questions: Where is your pussy getting the food? And how can I make it stop?

WHERE IS YOUR PUSSY GETTING THE FOOD

There are three traditional sources of food for pussies who cheat. They are:

1. Garbage Cans

There is not a garbage can in the world that a cheating pussy cannot get open. They do it by running lickety-split at the garbage can and butting it with their little heads until the garbage can falls over and the contents spill out. If you want to know if your pussy is raiding garbage cans, test its little head for big lumps.

WHERE IS YOUR PUSSY GETTING THE FOOD

2. Your Plate

Does this sound familiar? You're sitting down to your favorite dinner—whole roasted ox stuffed with fried chicken, candied yams, watermelon and a seventeen-layer cake, when you hear a sudden noise behind you. You turn to investigate, and when you turn back, the ox has disappeared. Surveying the room you can see nothing unusual, except for your pussy, who is lying in a corner panting slightly and farting and belching and sighing.

WHERE IS YOUR PUSSY GETTING THE FOOD

3. Wild Things

A desperate pussy is not particular about what it eats, and sometimes it will even resort to stalking wild game. It is easy to know if your pussy is stalking wild game. First, you will notice that the birdies have stopped singing in the morning. Then, you will not see your paper boy or your mailman anymore. Next, your neighborhood will take on the appearance of a ghost town as whole families begin to disappear. And finally, you will notice your pussy watching you everywhere you go, hungrily licking its lips and testing your flesh with its little paws.

WHAT CAN YOU DO?

What can you do with a pussy who cheats? Country singer Hank Slim says it best when he sings, "Trade in your pussy/for a Willy's Jeep/put your foot to the floor/and squash the little creep."

SIX WAYS TO INSURE YOUR PUSSY STICKS TO ITS DIET

Putting your pussy on a diet is one thing, but keeping it on a diet is something else. In order to keep your pussy honest, you must be cunning, resourceful, wise, vigilant, strong, mean and insensitive.

You must roar and claw and gouge and stalk and spit and be ready to kill or be killed. And this is just on the first day. After that, you can fall back on any one of these tried and tested techniques.

PUSSY DIETS

1. Calm Reason

(This almost never works.) When you and your pussy are seated side by side in armchairs, facing a crackling fire and sipping sherry and listening to the rain dance against the windowpanes, begin to explain why you think it would be a good idea if your pussy stayed on its diet. Argue as Epicures argued that moderation is good in all things. Argue as Socrates argued that flab makes reasonable men puke. Argue as Voltaire argued that you might not agree with your pussy's being fat, but you will defend to the death its right to lose weight. Be subtle, be sincere, be persuasive. And be careful not to pull the trigger of the loaded shotgun you are holding in your pussy's mouth, unless the little wretch tried to waddle from the room.

PUSSY DIETS

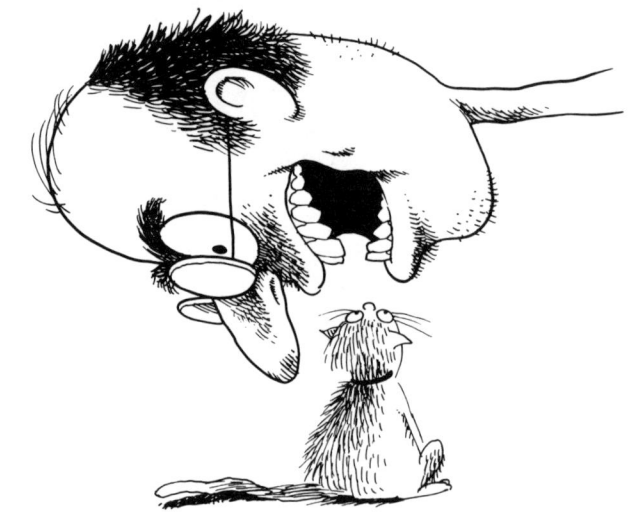

2. Shouting and Name Calling

Shriek at your pussy every time you see it. Be shrill and biting and sarcastic 24 hours a day. Demand to know when it is going to lose some weight already and stop embarrassing you in front of your friends. Demand to know when it is going to be slim and pretty like your friends' pussies. Demand to know why it hasn't married a doctor and got lots of money and fancy clothes like your friends' pussies have. Rant and rave and scream and moan and tear at your hair. Soon, both you and your pussy will have ulcers and won't be able to eat any more.

PUSSY DIETS

3. Use Sex As A Reward

There is an old Swedish saying. "A pussy in heat/don't want to eat." There is an old Russian saying: "A hot pussy doesn't take borscht to bed." There is an old Indian saying. "It's no fun making love to an elephant unless you're another elephant." There's an old Italian saying. "It's difficult to hold a pizza and a lover at the same time." There's an old Ethiopian saying. "Lasagna and lust don't mix." There's an old British saying. "Blubber belongs on whales." There's an old French saying. "What the hell, anything for a laugh."

PUSSY DIETS

4. Encase Your Pussy In Lucite

This way you can take your pussy with you wherever you go and not have to listen to it whimpering for food. And you can do lots of things with it. You can stand on it to get something off a high shelf. You can use it as a paperweight or a doorstop. You can even use it to crack walnuts. Be honest now. When was the last time you tried to crack a walnut with your pussy?

➤ PUSSY DIETS

5. Hypnotize Your Pussy Into Believing It Is A Fig

Figs are wholesome. Figs are nutritious. And when was the last time you saw a fat fig?

6. Make Your Pussy Hand Over Its Small Intestines

This is a drastic approach but an effective one. Tell your pussy you will give them back as soon as it swears off chocolate, fried foods, cream cheese, steroids, honey cocktails and blintzes with jimmies.

And if that doesn't work, whip up a batch of Pussy-a-la-King.

EXERCISING YOUR PUSSY

Any pussy that tries to lose weight without exercising is going to end up as a flabby pussy. And the only thing more undesirable than a fat pussy is a flabby pussy.

Ask any sailor.

So while your pussy is dieting, you must also give it plenty of exercise. There are two schools of thought on the way to exercise your pussy.

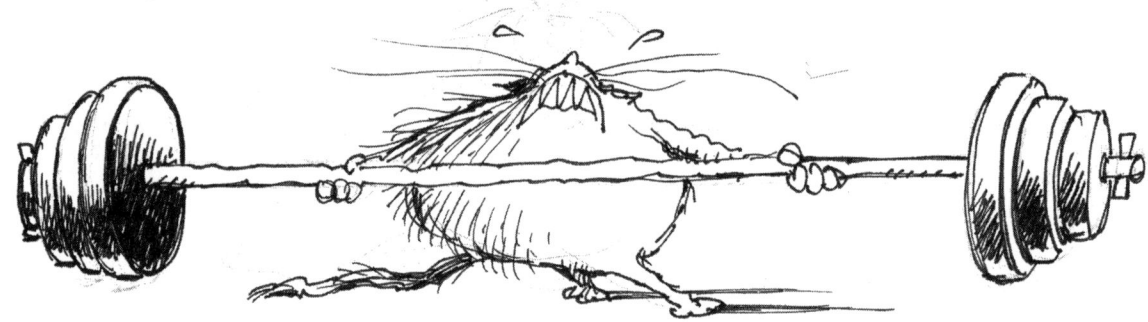

1. The Work-Up-To-It-Gradually, Logical and Reasonable Program

In this program you design a series of exercises for your pussy to do every day, starting with easy exercises, like "fetching kleenex," and working up to more difficult exercises, like "fetching anvils." You begin with a minute or two of exercises and gradually work longer and longer every day.

EXERCISING YOUR PUSSY

2. The Crash Program

In this program, which represents a somewhat more radical approach to pussy fitness, you lock your pussy into a cage with six starving bulldogs and a bottle of catsup. Believe me, at the end of five minutes, you won't even recognize your pussy.

Other books we publish are available at many fine stores. If you can't find them, send directly to us. $7.00 postpaid

2400-How To Have Sex On Your Birthday. Finding a partner, special birthday sex positions, kinky sex on your birthday and much more.

2402-Confessions From The Bathroom. There are things in this book that happen to all of us that none of us ever talk about. The Gas Station Dump, for example, or the Corn Niblet Dump, the Porta Pottie Dump and more.

2403-The Good Bonking Guide. Bonking is a great new British term for doing "you know what". Covers bonking in the dark, bonking all night long, improving your bonking, and everything else you've ever wanted to know.

2407-40 Happens. When being out of prune juice ruins your whole day and you realize anyone with the energy to do it on a weeknight must be a sex maniac.

2408-30 Happens. When you take out a lifetime membership at your health club, and you still wonder when the baby fat will finally disappear.

2409-50 Happens. When you remember when "made in Japan" meant something that didn't work, and you can't remember what you went to the top of the stairs for.

2411-The Geriatric Sex Guide. It's not his mind that needs expanding; and you're in the mood now, but by the time you're naked, you won't be!

2412-Golf Shots. What excuses to use to play through first, ways to distract your opponent, and when and where a true golfer is willing to play.

2414-60 Happens. When your kids start to look middle-aged, when software is some kind of comfortable underwear, and when your hearing is perfect if everyone would just stop mumbling.

2416-The Absolutely Worst Fart Book. The First Date Fart, The Oh My God Don't Let Me Fart Now Fart, The Lovers' Fart, The Doctor's Exam Room Fart and many more.

2417-Women Over 30 Are Better Because... Their nightmares about exams are starting to fade and their handbags can sustain life for about a week with no outside support whatsoever.

2418-9 Months In The Sac. A humorous look at pregnancy through the eyes of the baby, such as: why do pregnant women have to go to the bathroom as soon as they get to the store, and why does baby start doing aerobics when it's time to sleep?

2419-Cucumbers Are Better Than Men Because... Cucumbers are always ready when you are and cucumbers will never hear "yes, yes" when you're saying, "NO, NO."

2421-Honeymoon Guide. Every IMPORTANT thing to know about the honeymoon — from The Advantages Of Undressing With The Light On (it's slightly easier to undo a bra) to What Men Want Most (being allowed to sleep right afterwards without having to talk about love).

2422-Eat Yourself Healthy. Calories only add up if the food is consumed at a table. Snacking and stand up nibbling don't count. Green M&M's are full of the same vitamins found in broccoli and lots of other useful eating information your mother never told you.

2423-Is There Sex After 40? Your wife liked you better when the bulge above your waist used to be the bulge in your trousers. You think wife-swapping means getting someone else to cook for you.

2424-Is There Sex After 50? Going to bed early just means a chance to catch up on your reading or watch a little extra t.v., and you find that you actually miss trying to make love quietly so as not to wake the children.

2425-Women Over 40 Are Better Because... Over 90 reasons why women over 40 really are better: They realize that no matter how many sit-ups and leg raises they do, they cannot recapture their 17-year-old figures—but they can find something attractive in any 21-year-old guy.

2426-Women Over 50 Are Better Because... More reasons why women over 50 are better: They will be amused if you take them parking, and they know that being alone is better than being with someone they don't like.

2427-You Know You're Over The Hill When... You tend to repeat yourself. All the stories of your youth have already bored most acquaintances several times over. Even worse, you've resigned to being slightly overweight after trying every diet that has come along in the last 15 years.

2428-Beer Is Better Than Women Because (Part II)... A beer doesn't get upset if you call it by the wrong name; and after several beers, you can roll over and go to sleep without having to talk about love.

2429-Married To A Computer. You're married to a computer if you fondle it daily, you keep in touch when you're travelling and you stare at it a lot without understanding it. You even eat most meals with it. Truly advanced computers are indistinguishable from coke machines.

2430-Is There Sex After 30? By the time you're 30, parking isn't as much fun as it was in high school. He thinks foreplay means parading around nude in front of the mirror, holding his stomach in; and she has found that the quickest way to get rid of an unwanted date is to start talking about commitment.

2431-Happy Birthday You Old Fart! You're an Old Fart when you spend less and less time between visits to a toilet, your back goes out more than you do, you tend to refer to anyone under 40 as a "kid", and you leave programming the VCR to people under 25.

2432-Big Weenies. Why some people have big weenies while other people have teenie weenies; how to find big weenies in a strange town; rating a weenie; as well as the kinds of men who possess a putz, a prong, a schwanz, a member, a rod and a wang—and more!

2433-Games You Can Play With Your Pussy. Why everyone should have a pussy; how to give a pussy a bath (grease the sides of the tub so it won't be able to claw its way out); dealing with pussy hairs (shellac it so the hairs stay right where they belong); and everything else you ever wanted to know about pussies.

2434-Sex And Marriage. What wives want out of marriage (romance, respect and a Bloomingdale's Charge Card); what husbands want out of marriage (to be left alone when watching football games and to be allowed to go to sleep after sex).

Ivory Tower Publishing Co., Inc., 125 Walnut St., P.O. Box 9132, Watertown, MA 02272-9132 Tel: (617) 923-1111